THE MUSE OF LOVE & PAIN

a collection of dark poetry

A.X. SALVO

ABOUT THE AUTHOR

A.X. Salvo is the author of the international bestselling poetry collections _The Teeth Of The World Are Sharp, The Muse Of Love & Pain_, and _Devoured._

Salvo's writings and art have appeared in _USA Today, MISC, Studio Visit Magazine, Bete Noir, The Adroit Journal_, and _The Anthologist_. Salvo is also the recipient of a Vermont Studio Center grant for Poetry.

www.axsalvo.com
Instagram: axsalvo

THE MUSE OF LOVE & PAIN

Second Edition
Copyright 2020 © A.X. SALVO

CONTENTS

THE MUSE OF LOVE & PAIN: ACT ONE

THE MUSE OF LOVE & PAIN: ACT TWO

THE MUSE OF LOVE & PAIN: ACT THREE

THE MUSE OF LOVE & PAIN: ACT ONE

The Inevitable Pull

EVE

Leaving it an ashen white

I rob the sky of night

To behold the beauty closely

And give this wonder unto you

As I spread sugar

Over your lips

My fingers begin to quiver

Only moments ago a heavy, humid night

Soothed the surface of me

Cupped in my hands

At the mid of my palms

It blazes

The blackness rolls off me

Dripping down my fingers, droplets

Into your mouth

While you drink, thirsty for more

Leaning forward, eyes hungry for sight

I feel your longing for this genesis

Exude out your pores

Now the marvel is inside

Melting, mingling, blending

With the wetness of your

Tongue

Its intense gravity alters your own

A flood of truth

Far too many truths

Clarity pierces your mind like

Fangs

A mad poison burns through a stream

Reality

Brutal and ungodly

Sickens

I kiss you

Clenching your tongue

Between my teeth, as you seize

An hourglass frame

Convulses

Your sand spills

Every grain evanesces

Upon touching the ground

A death is nearly complete

The veneer is torn from

Those who have lied

Sin is known, understood, real

Now you are idle

Now you are my

Eve

RED ON WHITE

Lips on my cheek

Red on white

Lips in the darkness

Breathing sweet life

Lips around mine

Over and below

Lips of the silent soul

That I will never know

Lips like cherries, wild wind-swept berries

Falling into rivers

Lips healing my wounds

As I violently shiver

Lips press against my tears

Kill the pain

Lips in the storm

Swallow the rain

Lips the shape of two half moons

Beauty in the night

Lips into mine eyes

Blurring my very sight

Lips reflect the sun

Soft rose petals drink light

Lips delicate as innocence

On a face that is dove white

Lips forever shut

Hold divinity within

Lips deny evil

Hiding Eden from sin

Lips of the Queen of angels

Imprison a swift death

Lips prolong the suffocation

Of a broken man's breath

Lips so weak

Tremble at a touch

Lips rule my world

Eternity is not enough

Lips pull the sky out of space

The color of leather

Lips formed from rubies

Covered in feathers

Lips awaken dead hope

A soul rises beyond tomorrow

Lips devour a solemn past

Parting sweet sorrow

Lips mend my sanity

Stitching wounds within wounds

Lips free the golden butterfly

Lost in a cocoon

. . .

Lips consume Hell

Open wide the gates to peace

Lips murder every demon

Answering a fallen plea

Lips, lava red, on my flesh

Burn a message

Lips, summer hot

Leave a token, I caress it

Lips scorch the skin

Of a crying face

Lips waltz down my back

With passion and grace

Lips contoured with a devilish smile

Hint of what is to come

Lips tell a secret, centuries old

Of wars within, lost and won

Lips slowly descend

Smothered in fire

Lips sing dark poetry

Wrapped in wicked thunder

Lips I've not seen

For far too long

Lips I've not tasted

Since my love has gone...

QUIET

In her skin

He finds quiet

In her darkness

He finds solace

Complete and absolute

Warmth for one old cold man

Eyes darkened with lust pull him through time

Deeper deeper deeper still

Red locks pulling him back home

That safe place filled with song

That nest to memory and feelings numberless

. . .

All strung out, thirsty for her sex

Thirsty for her sweat, her salt and smell

Animal urge barking loud and angry

Hunger raw, hunger large

Like planets barren

Like starving orphans

He seeks comfort, her center

Lie down

Lie down

Shh...

YOUR STORM

I have come to conquer you dear

I will make the obvious clear

For long you've feared intimate love

The Devil held you down my Dove

He pressed his gun to your meek soul

Your graceful walk became a crawl

You vied for intermittent lust

Believing his actions were just

No matter what you bartered with

Or how much love you had to give

He taught you the same sad lesson

That inspired such deep depression

And he was the self-serving whore

You chose to touch, embrace, adore

Above all matters that mattered

While you stayed silent and battered

But I will no longer be silent

I will be strict, never violent

Too stubborn for a passive man

Too fragile for an unruly hand

You require a rare, simple cure

Born of a charming man's allure

Are you not ashamed, winded, and tired

Of being no one's desire?

Of being a borrowed lover?

An insignificant lover?

Turn your hurt into warm pleasure

I have the touch you are after

But you do not seek mere pleasure

You seek ecstasy, wild splendor

. . .

Soothe your red fervor with my lips

Devoured by a long, heavy kiss

Let us touch while we are able

Live as if life were a fable

Let us writhe and sweat while we still

Can, before we grow old and ill

Let our skin be our only friend

A sustenance no one could rend

Your mouth's moisture my sole milk

Your tongue, so thick, smooth seems of silk

How awful this crude punishment

To live without such nourishment

How terrible are the cravings, are

They not? So many nights alone

In the blue darkness of your home

Flesh begs for flesh, a flawless white

A brilliant, hypnotic sight

Imagine the rapture of your

Nude, slender glowing curvature

Over me, your torso held, thrust

Down onto me, this boiling lust

Shivers me, your hands clench wood with

An unnatural strength, as myth

Became possible for us

Your mouth stretched wide, a quick, hot gust

Of sexual breath, erotic

Music tumbling in narcotic

Trembles off our tongues

Your internal perfume fills my lungs

Lips surrounding the brown of your

Areola, blurring both your

Sight and your conception of bliss

These images are but a gist

Of what I may offer you dear

Wet me with your last, long held tear

Kneel over my form, let it fall

Into my eye, to see, know all

Your pains and pleas for affection

Your constant fights for attention

. . .

To Hell with useless oxygen

To Hell with food and cottages

The scent of a woman is all

I need to breathe to live, is all

That is needed to wake me, to

Awaken the drive to unglue

Myself from self-destructive acts

Make me handsome with your hands

Run your fingers across my face

Let me pay homage to your taste

To your pale, quintessential form

Let me dance with you in your storm

PALLID LUNAR MAIDEN

Pallid lunar maiden

With skin soft as crow feathers, as dawn's light

With eyes the color of wine, of quiet midnight

She wanders the avenues of my mind

To know the depth of her

May mean the death of me

For what other miracle

Would there be left to live

To know the subtle beauty of her morose thoughts

To know the creases of her palms

To count each lash upon her lids

To listen to every beat beneath her chest

To listen to the melodies from out each breath, the

Music, the lullaby that is her voice

To enchant, enthrall, engulf my entirety

BEYOND TOMORROW

Inevitable

Collision of souls

Defying

All laws others have told

Time

Circular in direction

Cycles of self-destruction

Breathe life into a prisoner

Once absolutely shattered

Our flesh meets before

Our fire breaches cores

Within fallen angels

Deep in God's cradle

We fuse

In a white-skinned caress

We dance

Till you lay without dress, without gown

Hot, uncovered mesh

Made of breath, of mirth

Before birth

You've known my name

The same you scream, you moan

Even alone

When only images greet you

Memories beseech you

To and fro and back

Across a black landscape

Which you've named Madness or

Candice, candy for short rather, for

But what sister is more sweeter

Than your shadow, the sleek and narrow

Silhouette

You've met in your dreams

Between the seams

Of your mind and my own

Where your tone of voice is shrill, ill

To me and no other

For, I under the torture

Fools and life have wreaked

Since you've begun to seek

The answers you desire

And I know you're so very tired

Of the stares

Of the slurs

And how it sometimes seems to blur

When thoughts come fast and heavy

Pain when you're not ready

To do it all again

In that circular direction

.   .   .

Find some solace in this truth

No matter how tight the noose

I will love you beyond tomorrow

Beyond the timelessness of sorrow

WHAT BLISS CAN BE

I would hate to lose evenings of

Sacred lovemaking

Near the fire

Burning embers after much

Sweet, red wine and

A decadent dance among the

Darkened trees of a midnight forest as

Winds grew fierce and distorted

Their shadows

Where we,

Shapeless, faceless

Danced to a silent song

Music we could not

Hear, but knew

Within the darkness of the

Shadow trees, until rare

Lightning revealed you

Embraced in

Rain

I would hate to lose mornings thereafter

Waking to the harmony

Of your bold beat

Of your calm breath

Waiting for your eyes to

Open and welcome

Me into

Love

Beauty

Heaven

I would hate to lose eyes

So gentle, such a

Soft brown, yet a

Sudden fiery red

Intense scarlet, alive

With the passion of our

Sacred act

I would hate to lose hands

Small, pale white as the

Feathers of the dove

That course my

Flesh

Scorching my

Skin with a

Sensual heat

I would hate to lose lips

So fragile

Such a delicate crimson, where

Bliss can be found in an

Angel's kiss

IMMOLATION

Chilled flesh beckons

From the center of

A deserted highway

Nimble fingers, slender fingers

Curl toward an

Unholy holy ghost

With blood as divine as mine

Within a frame

Brilliant and strong

As polished titanium

Tonight, I found

An ornate tapestry of

Scars

.   .   .

As we kiss

Our heads tilt

All is distorted

Bent beyond ourselves

Air escapes us

Wind elates us

Our breath shortens

Plays to the tempo

Beneath our chests

Quick-hard-heavy rhythms

Our lips twist, so too

Our minds

Our spines

Fierce mouths persist

Uncontrollable, rampant rapture

And I wish for nothing

But immolation

In your name

THE MUSE OF LOVE & PAIN: ACT TWO

Elusive Shadows

OPIATE PRINCESS

Pain killer

Where have you gone?

Kill the pain

Take its beaten corpse

And send it far down the river

They've masked every window

Locked ever door

They've taken my sight, I am

To see light nevermore

They've come to feed me lies again

They've come

To force me down

I am given seven scorpions

And told they are bread

I am given cursed hemlock

And told it is the blood of Christ

Poured from a chalice of lead

They break my skin

With the edges of my bones

Say this will rid me of disease

They inject sin into my veins

And name it medicine

You

Are my morphine

My beautiful, nightly opiate dream

Come, blanket me

With white warmth

Seep deep into my

Mind and blood

Bury me in a mountain of ivory

Feathers

Replace evil with love

Atrocity with divinity

I am cast into Hell

And told it is Eden

I can tell it apart

Because you are not here

They force me against wood

And say this must be done

They rob roses of thorns

To craft a crown

To be placed 'round my temples

To pierce each thought

Nails through the centers of

My palms

The same that once warmed your face

Grazed your lips

Shivered your back

Bolts through the nerves of my feet

Feeling more like lightning than metal

Thunder explodes across my mind

Pain

Strikes, stabs, sickens

While I cry blood and

Beg for more

Splinters tear my back and limbs

Whips and swears and screams surround

I howl

They smile

I bleed

They sing

I ask for truth

They say it is gone

I do not listen

Because you exist

EPIPHANY

Along the darkest cedar,

I reached for the raven

Desperate for his darkness, helpless

Gestures, thoughtless

But he was

Too far

Down the branch

Too close

To the edge

And I fell so very far, far

Too near the pyre

. . .

But you were there

Alabaster arms, marble hands

Reaching for my limbs which were

Truly bones

Awful, bleached things

You were there, but not to

Catch me, no you only wanted

To touch my flesh, my strange

Shadow like shape

Just once

Before I was impaled and ablaze

That is when I knew you

Were never meant to save me

But to be a witness to my fall

To my sacrificial ending

THE BELOVED

May I ask,

what is left of you?

Stains:

dried silhouettes of

tears and blood

shed for all you have lost and

all you will never have

Steel:

metallic within

glowing lava red

as the heart of Apollo's home

I watch the Nile

be poured from the hands of

gods

onto your naked corpse

to harden your innocence

to nourish your veins

to quiet that pain

weaken the screams

inside

Song:

a sonorous, lingulate voice

diving into me

wrapping me in the arms of a

divine caress

so very strong as to stop

the flow of breath

a rare, alembic voice

sent to rend

sin from my blood

The music off your gelid lips

this October night, with its full moon bright

reveals a certain lassitude

which we share

a perpetual malaise of the soul

provoked by ignorant men

you weep black rain

and so begins, a familiar song once again

the same that last rose me

out the dark sepulcher

the very chamber in which

man had imprisoned me

I was never meant to rest on the white

wings of my beloved Dove

never to listen to the bewitching

diminuendo

out her soul

as I gently lowered my eyes

farther than the Morning Star from Heaven

into the Great Deep

I fell, ever faster, ever sweeter

into a lengthy slumber

A melancholic drawl beckons

rings true and through the worn form

of a once lost roué

like Lazarus I rose

holy apparition of skin and blood

hands in the sky

she stood, my Christ

Stone:

static images, yet

still shifting, still trembling, of

forgotten selves

frozen in the past

false evidence of what once was

like the devout with statues of Christ

you worship the remnants of

what was not known

but only hoped to have been

When we pass through the gates

behold Death's features

intently look into his face

at his eyes, if he will have them

ask not at this moment

or the next wicked hour

that should befall you

the question

that drives us mad

wait till he is before us

then we will deny Heaven

refuse Hell

and demand Eden

HANDS

My thoughts consist of her giving hands

The translucent tones, the elegant beauty of

Little lines and blushed knuckles

Fragile bone of a woman who would save her

Killer before herself

I think of her fingertips and

How they speak to her; I wonder of

What they may have told her

What has her flesh spoken of?

What has it left unsaid?

Her fingers do not scream

They do not use words

They function with an ancient language

That only she knows

They speak to her

In a mad quiet with

Silent pictures that are at times

Horrible and tainted

Enough without the aid of sound or

Shrill voices

And I know every detail of this process

For I've endured the same

HARLEQUIN

I wish to rend the mask

From your front

I will carve my own

From the face of my former self

To be worn in the tragedy that is my

Present

And the comedy that was my past

Kill the beast

Kill the man

Let our souls burn!

They dare tame our fire

To lower the flames

In the name of

Fear and ignorance

In their cloudy eyes,

We are loathsome creatures

I will kiss the face of the

Soul I wish to call home

Until prisons collapse and

Lies fall

I will come to you

This fated night

To paint you in the

Colors of madness

Dove white

Around sharp, yet rotund cheeks

Kohl will surround

Blazing eyes and burning lips

All red with life and beauty

You become a true harlequin

We flee their world, their

Limits

Now, without human veneer

We stand

Without bones

Without flesh

We are only

Soul and blood

Behind nocturnal skins

Natural mass

Ask yourself

Are you free?

Yet?

ALONE

My eyes are locked

The room a blood black

Save the dim moonlight

Through the scarlet curtains

Waking the pale gray walls

A certain perfume hovers

It dances around me

Like a burning ballerina

A scent of baked apples

And summer wind

Though I am

In another's bed

In another's embrace

In another

I make love

To you

I kiss her lips

I taste your soul

I taste her flesh

I see your face

I rise into her

She exhales

With your breath

With your voice

She asks me to leave

Alone

I spend the duration of the night

With delusions of female grandeur

And a certain perfume

HOME

Where will you go?

When the snow begins to fall?

And your skin cries for warmth?

And your body cannot move forth?

Your flesh begs for flesh

Arms, where you can rest

Where will you roam?

Who is your home?

When your soul begins to weaken

All its elements slowly eaten

Leaving only darkness and sand

In the blackened palms of my hand

Here is what is left of you

Grain for grain, only I hold the truth

The answers you desire

The names of every liar

Who's denied you eyes

Who's raped your mind

Who's choked your soul with wire

And dared to quench your fire

Where will you find

Seductive, sacred blood

Poured from out the veins

Of he who knows your pains?

Yes, my porcelain dear

My blood will end your fear

Of death by awful thirst or lust

For, you drink not only blood, but life

Laced with trust

Only rapture, be it sinful or not, pervades

Divided, drowned, burned

It remains

MAGDALENA

This matter is delicate

the alabaster hands

the dark, perfumed strands

that wind around the

torso, lungs, and soul

that comfort and choke

to death

the pain of her patient

The meek curvature of docile lips

smiles abound

smiles abound

humble patience displayed toward

a struggling patient

whose veiled lacerations

are easily visible through her

pensive eyes and undoubtedly

under her analysis

Light spills from her mouth and pores

light pours, as she exhales relief

for he will soon rise

out his dim tomb

with no need for bandages

Reborn

in a new form

without his burdens

flesh unmarred, without scar

wings once black will glow

a blinding, burning white

and he will know absolution

through her gentle light

THE MUSE OF LOVE & PAIN: ACT THREE

Madness is Metamorphosis

GLASS TIGERS

Thoughts after midnight:

Morbid, macabre fantasies

Drift, strangle an already

Mangled man, as I

Much like the Devil

Fall an endless fall

Die and endless death through the

Glorious depths of a soundless canyon

Now,

Glass tigers riddle

My harrowed eyes

Whose pigments are now red,

Whose pupils are large and

Full of confusion

Yet,

The quiet cats are so careful

With soft steps, cautious intakes

Of my scent, with

Diamond noses below

Diamond eyes filled

With quiet flames

The quiet cats

Shift and shimmer still within

Awry absolution

In this nocturnal habitat

Among twisted vines of knowledge

Their aqua silhouettes, white stripes, and

Smoke breaths blur in a

Mad ballet of delicate motions

Brilliant claws tear and dance through

Black roses at my blistered toes;

Roses once as vivid a scarlet as could be

Found sleeping atop the

Fallow lips of the Muse to Love and Pain

Claws and purrs

Distract a boy from a different addiction

From the origin of his agony

Toward another direction

I love the menagerie surrounding me.

I love them - these creatures of instinct.

Though they are ruthless predators,

I love them

For the glass figures are

All that is left to be loved

My muse is gone

In a pitch room,

I plunge thin steel into the skin

Of my arm, once again

Needles numb wires, now altering

Blue hues

To a sickly brown

. . .

The Muse has made a

Dull heart hostile, a

Fractured heart quakes

Tumbles upward and

Shatters through my

Teeth and tongue

I cannot speak, yet

Dying with all the

Hollow of a shadow

My eyes sink into

Salt stung sockets

And they ask her:

Were you not to be my savior?

Now I find you a murderer

An enemy of sanity

A thief of beauty

For you, with your leave, have stolen

The last form of divinity

This world may ever know

She remains silent

And

I wonder

Of the tigers

I wonder

If anyone would add a crown to the collar

That steals my breath

The thorns disturb my voice, yet

Not my delusions

Yes, neither thunder, nor guns, nor shame

-*Nothing*

Could rob me from my daydreams

And I continue to wonder:

Was she ever really there?

THE INTANGIBLE

Burning and restless

A sable soul wanders, searches

For meaning, for what has

No name

No form

No taste, yet

She yearns to call

She longs to embrace

She craves to drink...

A thing with the

Texture of love

Flavor of life

Jubilance of youth

Spice of sin

Weight of despair

Gravity of death

Darkness of rage and

Irony of hope

An invisible tapestry woven by the

Hands of her Father

Crafted from strands numberless, of

Ebony memory, crimson pains, and white faith

A hot quilt with which she may warm a slender,

Alabaster body

Lovely, bare vampire skin

Nude, without scar, yet wounded

Thoroughly wounded

She roams alone

Pallid lids flutter

Long, black lashes curl toward cloudless night

A starless sky offers no answers

Wide, mahogany eyes are tilting down now

Stung with salt, laced with tears

Hollow orbs meet those of a child

A fetus floats in a dark pool

A thick, indigo amniotic lake

A fetus screams for his mother

Dreams of Heaven

Though it has never been there

Never seen where

Agony ends and bliss blooms

As an evening primrose beneath

A fragile moon

A fetus begs for his mother

Whose unmoving limbs, whose once lustrous

Flesh and red mane and daunting image

Reminds the quiet maiden of her own,

Before atrocity

The failing madam flickers thrice, parts her lips

To exclaim, but fades

Into the dying light 'round all

Mother is off now

Risen or fallen as far as the music

The waking corpse wishes to consume

. . .

She endures a second breath

Reaches for a son

Kisses the smallest lips,

Clutching them with her own

Milk flows from within, off her tongue and into

A new being, now full of time

She rids him of awful film with the

Rain out her aching orbs

Dries him with tender palms and gentle breaths

He no longer cries, but

Grows morphine-white wings

They allow flight beyond night, sight

Beyond clouds, beyond sorrow, and so he ascends

After wrapping himself around her beaming face

"Cherub fly, glide to Him, to destiny!" she cries

The son had left and taken with him

Warmth and light and glee

A lost apparition remains in vain

A familiar symphony beckons louder now

From every direction, nothing is linear

Perhaps all is circular?

She wonders, she ponders

She fears the angels' diminuendo

For it broods in an echo-like fashion

Far, yet near

Bright, yet dim

She fears she may never touch the songs

Though they cannot be held, only heard

A distant raven listens to confusion, silent hunger

An ashen woman thirsts for emotion

A mass of black feathers descends

She stands, eyes shut, waiting to be devoured

Mouth stretched wide,

Enough for the winged-shadow

To enter, yet it only leaves

A seed upon her wet tongue

The wise creature drops sin from its beak, while

A black blur blends into midnight

She cannot help, but swallow the apple origin

And so an evolution begins

Her brown spheres darken, harden

To the feel of steel

Diamond eyes shine, diamond eyes shine

With the most wicked color of wine

Anger fractures her eyes

From which blood now runs

Though she cries, no sounds escapes

Screams heard by her alone

Sparks dancing on her fingertips become flames

Smoke drifts, mixing with steam from each

Scarlet iris and blazing lip

Her shape abandons its form for one of

Porcelain

A break courses the mid of her back

Spiraling down her spine, up her neck

Black plumes gently extend through

Broken beauty

A divine choir is heard

A kaleidoscope of soft lights, a myriad of colors

Rend the few fragments left of her former self

Pain is evident, everlasting

Sweet, not bitter as before

Song is true, she knows the allure of

Epiphany, of glorious virtue

For she lives

Without name

Without form

For she stares at His eyes, or rather

Her reflection on them, though she has none

And sees the intangible

THE MUSE OF LOVE & PAIN

Far across the desolate sands

Beyond sight

A hot cry

Tore the silence of the desert

"Save a kiss for me"

She whispered to him, to only him

She spoke not words, yet he understood all the same

Though she had no language and

Spoke only music, a

Hypnotic song

To the melody of a somber violin, as if she were an

Instrument beauteous

He, and only he, knew

What she craved

Atticus rose from worn knees

Wild, black eyes toward the horizon, and

Ascended a wicked hill,

Heavy thirst

Thick heat

Mocking mirages of divine oases, and

Apathy from the sun

Slowed his pace

Ferocious winds took strict hold

Forcing dust into his face, via an

Awful gust

Blurring his vision

Tears flowed in abundance

Yet forward he went

Till a sudden haze crushed his mind

Shutting the gates to thought

Atticus lost the war against

The developing darkness and

Soon fell into a great slumber

. . .

"Save a kiss for me"

Gentle notes chimed inside him

Atticus awoke amid a darkening wood

Pink, blue, green, red, orange, and golden-leafed

Sequoias denied an

Angry sun

"I must taste her voice," said Atticus

As he rested a tired frame against course timber that

Stretched the limits of the powder blue sky, from which a

Fragile dove descended, and violently

Fluttered around Atticus, who

Froze at the sight of its

Bloodstained belly, and

Locked his eyes, and

Gave his back to

Marred beauty

A quick rip in the fabric of dead sound, like the

Launch of a steel arrow

Shot against the grand tree

Crashing its gravity into the face and

Limbs of Atticus

"Save a kiss for me," she whispered louder

Neither a broken face, nor exposed bone could

End him

Atticus grasped the ax embedded into the mid of the mighty tree and

Cut through its layers until a division brought

Freedom

Once again, Atticus rose

Forward he went, where

Growths of fogs masked a home to

Black widows decorated with

Scarlet hourglasses on their backs, offended

Scorpions with dancing tails, and

Fierce droves of black and gold

All in discord with Atticus

Caught in the gossamer maze, he

Fought the fury of stings and bites with a

Hurricane velocity, as they

Pierced skin like a thousand

Syringes

Atticus crawled through the storm, as the

Hush of twilight

Ate the horrid gray and brought

Peace

An odd shadow grew from out the earth

Two massive forms of black

Glass, the shape and texture of

Raven wings

Extended across the length of the winter forest

Atticus ran swollen hands across the

Smoothness of the endless wings

He peered at the root, where the two met, from which they were

Born, and charged forward

Shards stuck into and spliced through flesh, the

Abandoned halves shattered into

Infinite mirrors

Ebony fragments of truth

Distorted reflections, and

Reminders of the present

Failing breath

Hunger and nausea choked him

"Save a kiss for me"

"I must have your lips," answered Atticus

Lightning struck his center, an

Onslaught of scolding rain

Hammered upon his crown

Atticus tasted salt on his tongue with each

Tear the sky shed, his

Wounds burned

Blood boiled

Vapor rose off his body

Pain surged through exhausted nerves, as he

Roared in agony and ran, until he

Escaped the torrential barrage of

Lucid bullets

An expanse of

Torture now welcomed him

Rows upon rows, columns and columns of

Red roses completed an infinite garden

It towered over him, its

Malicious shadow seemed to smile

Atticus raced through the

Ocean of thorns, while they

Devoured his

Bones of skin, his

Skull of a face, and grew

Blacker till their

Deadness became ashes

Blown into nothingness by the

Muse of Love and Pain

"Save a kiss for me"

There, before him

Tall and sleek

Stood a miracle

An image of naked perfection

Who cast no shadow

While feathers circled 'round her

Upon her crown flowed fire

A vivid, marvelous mane composed of

Brilliant strands of flame that withstood the

Cold and bitterness of the winter night

Her eyes

Dark and deep

Shone with a seductive blend of

Crimson and mahogany

The color of blood with caramel

Bold and sweet as

Holy wine

Each iris held ancient secrets within its

Alembic sea

Into which he wished to wade

Skin crafted of snow

Embraced her soul

"I crave your skin," whispered Atticus

Indigo lips adorned with

Diamonds awaited him

The Muse wrapped icy fingers around his front and

Pressed pale lips into him

Such a cold kiss, yet it felt as if

Lava, not blood, coursed his veins

His mind became fogged by lust

He drank her like a river

She became the chalice

From he would drink the

Fountain of life

The Muse beamed

. . .

As if a second bolt had struck, Atticus leapt back in

Awe, he

Looked at his legs, then his

Hands and traced his face with them

Skeletal remains were no longer felt

Every wound healed in a moment of bliss

The Muse of Love and Pain

Crossed her ivory hands, and

Cupped each cheek, to

Kiss Atticus once again

She pressed harder

Drowned in a supple rapture, a

Narcotic rush burned through him, a

Morphine-like veil encompassed reality

Psychosis wound through him in a liquid vertigo

She swallowed the life from his eyes, making them white, the

Darkness of his flesh morphed into light, and his

Heart froze into red ice

The Muse of Love and Pain left

Atticus and raised her lips to the night to

Inhale the stars and

Threw his soul to the sky

Cast black with the shadows of the dead, and so

He learned

The brevity of life

FOREVER WHITE, FOREVER BLACK

Born into a world that never wanted her, she roams the desolate, back alleys of a broken city. Ash white, without flaw, her form flows apparition among the living, glowing with unholy light, she moves unseen. An alizarin tint escapes her pores a black leather trench-coat embraces her slender frame like a dark skin of ink, second to only her own. Cold to the touch, yet hot against her flesh, it clings like a ravenous lover to his prey. Like her beloved Raven.

She treads with black boots that reach just over her knees and lick the streets swollen with rain. Her breast quiver at the strength and chill of the October winds, for she is nude, save the leather around her narrow torso - below her barren throat, burning lips, holy arch, and sharp ankles. Her shadow slightly lies and forebodes a seven foot demon. A six foot figure with strawberry-blonde curls around cheeks kissed with a red flaming vengeance quietly emerges out of the depth of midnight. Her soul holds a form so very black and twisted with pain that only one imbued with an equal madness could mend her.

Tonight, she searches for those who have sinned. She runs into a field of screams, to lay carnage without thought, without feeling, only passion for justice. A raging numbness at her center that is lodged for eternity; to last even after death when her own evil will be judged.

In the city, in the night, inside its bleeding womb, she waits for the growth of fangs to enable a feast of poison from every vein of its population. She wants to drink sin, to taste its bitter sweet wickedness in a lovely intoxication. For when that bleak shroud swallows the tenderness in everything, and all has succumbed to the psychosis of silent sound - broken only by howls and bullets - the innocent, even the innocent become guilty. She knows what occurs, what devils are conjured when the blackness drapes the blind and forces sight and their fanciful fantasies are eroded down to nothing. Yes, she knows the horror. It had already taken its toll on her, demanding an unending thirst for bloodshed when the moon emerges.

"No!" the fools yell. For a moment, they are allowed a single word, only a burst of syllable. She tears the lips from their faces, the tongues out their mouths, along with several teeth of her choosing. All with only her icy fingers. She laughs a mad, shrieking laugh that spirals up to the starless sky; a cacophonous whirl off her gleaming tongue. Oh, how wonderful it was to have her hunger quenched; if only for one night. Her craving for violence, the cracking of bones, the cries of mercy always falling on uncaring ears - it would rise again.

Her fiery strands hug her neck as she crosses into an unlit avenue creating a black-white fringe, blurring passed brick laden buildings and flaming trash cans. Rain seeps in the deadness of her scarlet mane. She loves the coldness she feels every moment a loose hair touches her collar bone, reminding her of how her nerves must feel. If only she could touch them also, to be galvanized by her own electricity, by the lightning within herself. Perhaps then, she would fall apart to be reassembled in the gardens of Eden. Perhaps in a more fragile form with white feathers and rounded beak.

But the cold did not last. Her rendezvous with divinity is severed, as her peerless eyes sink into themselves, widening with surprise.

He stands before her, close enough to hear her heart sing. Ringing louder than his, which was now changing its rhythm to a rather fierce music. Head-to-toe in black and rain, he dons a costume similar to hers. A small, almost unseen smile bends his purple lips. Almost unseen to any other; she knows he smiles and why.

She lunges at his throat, lips spread to meet his jugular. His body locks, rocks against brick then concrete as they drop onto the road. Pinned by her, his eyes roll far back into his mind as if her wet tongue had secreted morphine from its tip. Every muscle inside him tightens, fibers contract in a grand spasm, a sweet ache biting every nerve in his being as an erotic shiver flows, weakening his legs. Her indigo lips clench the flesh of his neck harder. She sucks with a violent pull, darkening the paleness of his skin. Lingulate waves push against an essential rope filled with life. Her jaw stretches, her eyes open to behold the ecstasy boiling in his.

The storm grows angry. Trees are torn from the ground. Yet she continues to devour him thinking of random excursions. Recollections of hot revolvers; spent pistols releasing smoke and souls. Memories of blades across and into loathsome creatures, of the ignorant and drowning. Those who never loved her shared the same fate. She sliced them into all sorts of shapes. Sometimes, she would merely tap them about the temples with the tips of her fingers, revealing the gravity and agony of her past. The horrid images would streak across the landscape of their hopeless, limited minds, charring their innocence, scorching them with her madness. The worst, the most vile, were mashed into a thick soup of mangled bone and shredded skin. She rendered them with strikes from metallic fists, steel knuckles. She beat into them with a golden glory that sat, unmoving on the surface of her iris.

He rips her from her dreams, her lucid visions and great conquests with a sleight of hand. He reaches underneath the back of her leather gown to count each rigid vertebrae of her spine with gelid fingers. One for every eon he loved her. He roams around to the skin upon her ribs and strokes them in a gentle motions; a tender strumming as if they are the strings of a violin. She moans, filling with a narcotic tremble, her face and body flush with a heat, an unnatural heat. The air surrounds and gnaws at their bones, yet the fire within them burns ever sweeter, ever faster, and ever hotter. He wraps quivering lips around her, tasting the darkness, the depth of lost shadows, reaping all evil in this reflection. He feels the bliss of Heaven and rage of Hell in a clean second. Every ounce of hate, of obsession, and malice writhes throughout his soul from hers.

A flash of blinding white awakens the sky. A low thunder follows. A second bolt descends, crashing into their oblivious forms, burning through the souls of a fallen angel dyad. They fuse, flesh bone blood, in a last caress - knowing this is the death of them. Subdued by the night, seduced by the city, they thrive in more fragile forms. One soars with feathers white as smoke, the other with dark plumes - black, forever black.

CUT

Now I kneel here

at her grave

wondering

which words to say

I sensed this loss

so long before

that sad, slow knock

came at my door

Now I lay here

in the snow

shaking

naked

and alone

I'll cut myself

and bare my bones

until I see

her perfect ghost

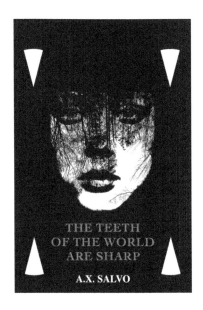

KEEP READING THE TEETH OF THE WORLD ARE SHARP

"I have never seen a more hauntingly beautiful book. It is a wonderful collection of poems and art that cuts deep from a place of tragedy and love."

AVAILABLE NOW IN PAPERBACK AND E-BOOK

THANK YOU

I dedicate this collection to all of my exceptionally beautiful family, friends and readers. I can't express how much I truly appreciate you.

Thank you all for supporting an independent writer and helping me do what I love.

If you enjoyed **THE MUSE OF LOVE & PAIN,** please take a moment to rate the book on Amazon and/or Goodreads.

Explore my other books.

The Teeth Of The World Are Sharp
An illustrated collection of dark art and poetry inspired by Edgar Allan Poe, Sylvia Plath, Neil Gaiman and the horror manga of Junji Ito. *The Teeth Of The World Are Sharp* explores trauma, abuse, death, grief, and loss. Each poem is carefully illustrated with haunting black and white drawings

Where I End And You Begin
In this fourth collection of poems, Salvo takes you deeper into

the shadows and delivers another brutally emotional experience with even more of what readers loved from his bestselling book *The Teeth Of The World Are Sharp* with more than 150 pages of new poems and hauntingly beautiful black and white drawings that blend dark fantasy, myth, and horror.

Beautiful Shadows

An illustrated anthology of dark art and classical poetry that includes famous poems by Poe, Neruda, Frost, Keats, and many others!

Devoured

Devoured is an exploration of the pleasure and the pain that can only come from love. I wrote this book of poems for all the souls who wander with shattered hearts.

Pretty Hate Machine

A macabre horror/sci-fi tale told from the monster's perspective. *Pretty Hate Machine* introduces us to the trials of Orion. The ruthless beast that stalks the streets of the dystopian Chaoxte in search of human prey.

Printed in Great Britain
by Amazon